To the great
Lady Lil —
a genius and
friend. —
Love
Bridwell

Mount Horeb

Mount Horeb

RUSSELL BIRDWELL

Illustrations by
Frances Hernandez Cunningham

Robert Speller & Sons, Publishers, Inc.
New York, N.Y. 10010

Library of Congress Catalog Card No. 77-187991
ISBN 0-8315-0122-7

First Edition

Printed in the United States of America

For those who believe in
miracles
and are aware of them

*"I have been driven to my knees
many times by the overwhelming fact
I had no other place to go."*

Abraham Lincoln

MEMO FROM THE AUTHOR

Not long ago a friend, a surgeon, proud of a technique he had developed for brain surgery, invited me to witness a delicate operation on the brain of a young girl.

At six o'clock one morning in a hospital in a seacoast town near Los Angeles I walked into surgery gowned in white and with a mask over my nose and mouth. I stood close enough to the operating table to be under the glare of the bright lights that bathed the patient. For a long while, as the exposed brain of the girl lay bare beneath the surgeon's scalpel, I felt I was in the presence of an infinite world; yes, in the presence of eternity.

And when I could gaze no longer at immortality, I looked about the white room. My eyes above my mask saw another pair of eyes, looking steadfastly and quietly upon the operation. Although he was the only other onlooker in the room—except the nurses—I had been unaware when he came in. His were the bluest eyes, the quietest eyes I had ever seen. I couldn't forget them; they had a haunting, serene quality.

After the operation I went to the surgeon's office. The stranger with "the eyes" was shaking hands with the doctor.

"Thank you, Doctor," I heard him say. "I'll know when to return. I will know when you need me."

The stranger turned to go and my friend introduced me.

"I want you to meet John Ericson," the surgeon said.

We shook hands, Ericson said nothing, smiled pleasantly, then walked down the hall and disappeared.

I looked after him, fascinated by what he had said to the doctor: "I'll know when to return. I will know when you need me."

"That was an odd thing for him to have said. Who is he?"

The doctor answered me as if he were speaking to himself. "Who is he?—I don't really know. All I know is that his name is John Ericson and he is the most extraordinary man I have ever known. All I truly know is that whenever I face difficult surgery—especially with children—he is always there in the operating room. He comes and goes very quietly—and usually says nothing. I do not know how he knows when he should come. But when I need him I look around the room and he is there."

And then the surgeon told me about John Ericson's friends—Captain Riis and First Mate Samuelson and Matt Trevins—the most incredible story I have ever heard; a story so strange that I have never told it before.

Here I have tried to put it down on paper as it was told to me that morning, a little after dawn . . .

—Russell Birdwell

Part One

THE BEGINNING OF A JOURNEY

*"Except ye see signs and
wonders, ye will not believe."*
John 4:48

The rain came in a heavy and steady downpour but it was doubtful if the hatless man who was groping his way on staggering legs through the early morning dark was even aware of it. The bullet wound in his right side—the lead still imbedded midway between armpit and waist—throbbed through him with stabbing pain and the thought never left his mind that with every successive step he was losing a dangerous amount of blood. Moving against the rain, he gritted his teeth and staggered on.

Presently he'd come to O'Regan's flat, at East 54th Street. Doc would take care of him. For his own security Doc wouldn't make a report to the police. As a consequence the press wouldn't hear about it. Often he had treated O'Regan with derisive contempt. Now he cursed himself because he had failed to appreciate O'Regan—a brilliant man who had been barred, years before, from practicing his profession in open society.

Matt stopped suddenly in the middle of the sidewalk and looked searchingly about him. This was a street he knew, but it was not the one that led to O'Regan's flat. He had been stumbling blindly in the wrong direction; somewhere, back there, he had taken a wrong turn. Steadying his trembling body against a building, clenching his fists as though in a fresh call for strength, he realized he had crossed Broadway west on Sixth. The Hudson River was not too far away. I've been walking longer than I imagined, he said to himself. He had gone by Madison Square Garden and he had not even been aware of it.

He guessed that it was about four o'clock in the morning. He had not passed more than one or two pedestrians or seen a single roving taxicab. Even in the greatest city in the world the silence and the dark could be like that of any nine o'clock town. He felt grateful for this because he did not want to be accosted in his condition by a policeman.

Without knowing why, he continued to walk in a westerly direction. The pain grew more intense; he had the fearful awareness that he was gradually growing weaker; and he was suddenly appalled by the thought that in all his life he had never been as deserted or more lonely than now. The thought sent a racking fear through him—he who had boasted that he was above the common fear. In his own way he had reckoned himself an important man. All the money he had could not save him—if death lay immediately ahead.

Where in hell am I going? he said to himself, suddenly. And why am I heading this way? The sound of the silent words rang loudly in his blurred consciousness and he felt a growing irritation because he was without an answer.

He didn't know why he was walking straight toward the river. It occurred to him that the neighborhood was vaguely familiar—a shabby tenement district. Crumbling red brick cold-water flats, empty warehouses, dingy store fronts. On one of these mean streets he had been born and spent the greatest part of his boyhood. Always he had carried in his heart a grim and bitter memory of those years.

A hacking cough started and he bent over double to better gain his breath, feeling the rain pelting down on his water-soaked clothing and bare head. If he dropped down on the sidewalk in sheer misery and weakness no one would see him until daylight. He'd be a headline in an afternoon newspaper —MATT TREVINS SLAIN! An ironic ending to a life . . . a man who had risen from the gutter, had gone back to the gutter to die. The newspapers would make something of this.

With an effort of will Matt drew on a last reservoir of strength and continued walking toward the river. Something in him cried out in a warning. He was unable in his weakness, fear, uncertainty, to understand its meaning; he realized only that there was a force stronger than himself that urged him irresistibly forward. The image of the river was in his mind's eye: the wide waterfront streets, the murky dark water, the ships at anchor, the deep, cavernous sheds containing merchandise from all parts of the world.

In the welter of emotion Matt was afraid; suddenly, horribly afraid of Death. Not of dying. Of Death, he said to himself. There was a difference. One might be the cessation of all knowing, the other was a thing of conscience which would never give him peace. It didn't matter that the thoughts were blurred—he knew they were—but they were nevertheless real, too, because no man cares to come face-to-face with the realization that he is to die the next minute. In the gutter. In the rain. Like a mongrel cur.

Weakness overcame him; he stopped, looked around, then shuffled to the edge of the sidewalk. He sat down heavily, painfully on the curb. He cupped his face in his hands and let the rain run down his neck on the cold wet skin.

The image of Joe Carlos sprang up in front of him, a grimacing, laughing devil of a man. Matt hated him. The feeling was violent inside him. He hated Joe and he hated Nancy. God, damn them both, he swore to himself.

Pal Joey. Matt's confidant. Matt had seen to it that Carlos, a struggling ward-heeler, was declared a candidate for State Senator. The nomination was tantamount to an election. In turn, Joe served Matt as a lobbyist at Albany. In a lush period of three years Joe had grown sleek, confident, too cunning in matters of money and with an eye for a pretty woman— even if the woman was someone else's property. Matt had no inkling of Carlos' duplicity until a few hours ago. He had telephoned Carlos, told him to come over.

"What do you want to see me about at this time of the morning?" Carlos demanded.

"Don't ask questions," Matt said. "Get up here right away!"

There was a silence. Then Carlos' steady voice came again.

"All right. Nancy is with me—we'll both come."

With the rain beating down on him, Matt Trevins relived the scene. Nancy Morrison was golden, tantalizing bitchery —for over two years she had held Matt captivated. Standing in the living room of his apartment, Matt realized that she no longer belonged to him.

"Okay, Matt, you see I'm not afraid," she said. "I'm not afraid of you anymore—and you can't do anything about it."

Nancy Morrison was more than an elegant body—she possessed a capable, cool mind. She was Carlos' brain—and more: she was Carlos' courage.

Matt spoke smoothly, "Come to think of it, you and Carlos deserve each other—whore begets pimp."

Suddenly there was a gun in Carlos' hand. Then the shot, the blasting pain in Matt's side.

Nancy Morrison looked down at Matt on the floor and said coldly, "If you live, you're not going to do anything—to Joe or to me. Good-by, Matt. I hope you die."

After they were gone Matt looked at himself in the bathroom mirror—blood was pouring from the wound and his face was convulsed with pain. He made an effort to stem the blood, even as he tried to plan his next move.

He called his secretary, Rose Henry, but no one answered. Then he found Doc O'Regan's private number.

A whiskey-hoarse voice said, "Sure, Matt, you come on over. I'll be okay by the time you get here."

The rain increased with new fury and Matt shook his mind free of the apartment. A fog horn sounded in the distance. Long and mournful, it was like the plaintive cry of someone dying.

He got to his feet with great effort. His soggy shoes, like dead weights, dragged on the pavement. The fog horn sounded again, this time short and heavy.

"I want to live!" Matt raged aloud. "Oh, God, help me!"

He was startled at himself. He was not sure it was his own voice. Then, suddenly, with a new strength he spat out defiantly, "For what am I begging?" It isn't, he argued with himself, that I'm afraid of dying. It's the dying in the street, not a man nor a woman in the world caring a damn. It's a rotten, miserable finish. If it weren't for his expensive tailored suit of gray flannel and the roll of currency in his pocket— he carried no identifying papers—he might be just another stiff on a slab at the morgue. He staggered forward, coughing, breathing heavily.

The image of Ruth, his wife, came back to him. In her days of dying she had told him: "It can't be the great loneliness which some people say it is; for in the thing we call Death there surely cannot be any suffering; there must be only a great release, an exchange for something wonderful, the last adventure for which the first was only a beginning."

The invocation of her name gave him a feeling of sadness. A memory of something that should have been very fine and was not because Matt Trevins was what he was, a man who had always believed that in order to make your way you had to fight hard, never to expect or give quarter, never to believe in charity; sometimes never to believe in decency. Life was a tough go, all the way down the road to the finish line.

The finish line. The words had a sickening finality. "God, give me another chance, a break, or whatever You call it. Please help me!" he cried.

Suddenly he had an impression of a big shed coming into his line of vision, a blur of lights and a taste of rain water in his mouth. He stumbled; his hands touched mud, grime, street refuse. . . .

He felt the hard impress of hands that caught him and lifted him onto his feet. A voice spoke to him.

"I shall help you."

It seemed to Matt in the last moments of consciousness that the voice, gentle and reassuring, was unlike any voice he had ever heard.

Throb and beat, throb and beat; a rhythmical surging energy vibrated through his body.

Presently the throbbing disassociated itself from him to become the sound of a ship's engines. He opened his eyes

slowly. He was in a small room. Directly across from his bunk there was another bunk and, above it, a porthole. The second bunk, neatly made up, was empty. Through the open porthole the sun poured in, strong and clear. Matt realized that the ship was moving through a calm sea.

A light blanket covered him. Lifting it, he saw that he was wearing a white surgical jacket. He drew it up above his waist. Where the bullet had ripped into his flesh there was now only a slightly reddish discoloration, as though the wound had never been real. The skin lay naked and unbandaged.

Matt sat up. He felt a slashing pain. That, at least, was real. But the pain was of short duration. Experimentally he put his legs out, then he stood up. His eyes moved slowly about the monastic room; a room, Matt figured, that probably belonged to a ship's officer.

His gaze was held by the burning light of a tall white candle in a silver candelabra standing on a table beside the second bunk. There was a rare color about the candle flame; steady and refined, it seemed to Matt that it possessed an ethereal quality, a kind of immortality, like that of the candlelight which burns, day and night, before the tomb of the Unknown Soldier on the Champs Elysee in Paris which Matt had admired not so many years before.

The door opened and a man stepped lightly into the room.

He said, "Hello, sir," in a quiet voice. He was about Matt's age, a little taller, and attired in a blue shirt and a pair of faded dungarees. He was bareheaded. His hair was dark and his features rugged. His smile was warm, friendly.

Matt said, hesitatingly: "This ship . . ."

"Mount Horeb."

"I had a bullet hole, right here, in my side," Matt continued. "Who operated on me?"

"The captain."

"The captain?" Matt was startled. "The captain operated on me?

"This is the strangest thing I've ever . . ." Matt broke off.

"Not a scar. This man must be one of the world's . . ." Again he cut himself short. "Is this the truth you're telling me? The captain of this ship . . ."

"He is also a surgeon," the man said quietly.

"What's his name?" Matt asked abruptly.

"Riis."

"I want to thank him. I'll pay him for the operation. I'll pay him ten times his fee."

"He has no fee."

Matt stared at the other. "Why would he do this?"

"You don't know our captain."

"What kind of a ship is this?"

"A freighter."

"Where are we heading?"

"The West Coast."

"Where are we now?" Matt asked.

"We just left Charleston."

Charleston, South Carolina; that was quite a jump from New York. To Matt is seemed fantastic that he had no recollection of the time that had disappeared.

He gave the sailor a sharp, quick look. "I don't mind telling you I don't understand any of this. It just doesn't add up. Can you explain it to me?"

"Yes—God."

Matt was silent. He listened to the sound of the ship's bell, listened to the beat of the engines.

The sailor smiled—a smile which seemed to dissolve the tenseness.

"Come to think of it, I haven't introduced myself. I am John Samuelson. First mate. You and I are sharing this cabin."

"I'm Trevins—Matt Trevins."

"Yes, I know."

"How did you know my name?"

"You told the captain when you came aboard."

It seemed a curious thing to Matt that Samuelson's poise, an air of calm and strength which he exuded, reassured Matt considerably that all was well.

"What's our next port?"

"Panama City."

"That's where I'll get off," Matt said, as if it were an announcement.

"That is up to you."

Matt gave Samuelson a sharp look. "What do you mean by that? Is there any reason why I can't get off?"

The mate's gaze was steady, and Matt even detected a gleam of amusement in the dark eyes. "I'm sure the captain will be able to answer your questions."

"When am I going to see him?" Matt's voice sounded almost like a challenge.

"He's looking forward to meeting you."

Matt's trousers lay over a chair beside the bunk. He picked them up, reached into a pocket, and felt the roll of money he had carried with him.

"You will have no need of money on this ship," Samuelson smiled.

"I will when I get off," Matt said with good humor as Samuelson started for the door.

For a while Matt lay on the bunk, his hands under his head, and concentrated on one thought—the time that he would leave this ship and fly to New York.

Of one thing he was sure—the day he got back he would square accounts with the two people he hated most in the world—Carlos and Nancy.

Night had fallen when Matt awakened from a restful sleep. He was alone. The candlelight provided the same rare glow in the room. The porthole was closed and on a table near him he saw a tray on which there was food—milk, cheese, crackers and an assortment of fruits. Matt ate heartily, enjoying every bite.

The ship was plowing through a calm sea. He heard voices outside in the passageway. It gave him a sense of activity in a world into which he felt himself unaccountably immersed: The captain-surgeon whose face he had not yet seen, whose hands he could not remember. The candlelight, forever burning. The silence.

Matt decided he had had enough of the cabin. He was excited by the resiliency he felt, the physical power coursing through his entire body. It was wonderful. He stood up. He was strong. His side didn't hurt. Still in his hospital gown he tried walking. He took the first steps carefully. No trouble. Call it a surgeon's miracle or God's act, anything, it doesn't matter, Matt said to himself. What matters is that he felt good. He wasn't weak any longer. He found his clothes. He dressed. He was Matt Trevins. Alive!

The cabin door opened into a companionway. It was lighted by a beam of yellow light from a small electric bulb. Matt climbed some stairs to the deck. He saw no one and he proceeded aft. He noticed that there was, strangely, not a sign of a single lifeboat. A light shone from an open door. Matt glanced in—he could see that it was the radio shack. There was no one inside. He glanced up the deck. Another cabin rose directly forward to starboard, its porthole gleaming. Matt walked up to it. The door was closed. He rapped on it lightly. There was silence. He knocked again, louder.

"Come in," a voice said.

Captain Riis sat in a large chair by a desk. He was a tall and angular man. In his white singlet and blue trousers, with dark brown hair and a Vandyke beard touched with gray, he seemed at first almost austere. But his large blue eyes, set wide apart under the dome of forehead, regarded Matt calmly. His face was burned by suns and winds. His voice was precise.

"Please sit down."

Matt eased himself into a chair. A few papers were spread on the table and the ship's log was open.

"Sir, I want to thank you for the job you did on me."

The captain smiled. "We are happy to have you with us. It should be a good journey."

Matt felt his heart beat faster. The word *journey* rather than *trip* baffled him. He wondered if there was a hidden meaning in the use of the word.

"The truth is, sir, I hadn't planned on a sea voyage." Then Matt grinned, qualifying hastily: "I hadn't planned on any kind of a trip. I'll get off at the next stop."

"Why are you in such a hurry?"

"Business," Matt said.

"It can't wait?"

"No," Matt said tersely.

"I think it would do you good to stay with us for awhile."

Matt decided on boldness. "Tell me, Captain. Am I a prisoner on this ship?"

"Prisoner?" The captain repeated the word softly. He smiled. "No. You are not a prisoner. You are a convalescent."

"Why did you do this for me?" Matt looked at the captain intently.

"It was an order."

Matt couldn't help his momentary start. "An order? Who from?"

"God," Riis said simply.

Matt struggled to hide any outward sign of disbelief in Riis' explanation. A concept of God had always struck him as something which belonged to the holy Joes, priests and ministers; to frighten people and to make them hew to a common line, each according to his own pattern. Maybe a man was better for his religion, but he knew plenty of men who had no religion at all and they had done all right.

Not until the night he had pitched forward on the wet sidewalk by a pier had he, Matt Trevins, done any business with the Lord. Could there be such a thing as a Power speaking to Riis and capable of issuing an order to pick up a wounded man at a certain time and a certain place?

In his Sunday School days, Matt recalled, he had been told of people who had a nodding acquaintance with God but no one had gone so far as to say he was being given specific orders on a timetable basis. His father, whom Matt barely remembered, didn't believe in anything; his mother never questioned any part of the Holy Writ. And Matt was interested solely in coming to grips with the outside, tangible world.

His first job had been as a copy boy on the old World-Telegram. From the lips of reporters he heard of police captains who had bank accounts by far exceeding the savings from their respective paychecks; of racketeers growing ever more powerful, wealthy, respectable after a fashion; of venal politicians who were no less respected or feared. To become a powerful guy in some racket where the opportunities for making money were great—that became Matt's obsession.

He moved fast. He got a job as a clerk in the office of the New York Park Commissioner. He attended night school, graduated, then obtained a position as secretary to the Commissioner himself. He was moving up in the world.

When he was twenty-four he married Ruth Bigby, the daughter of a ward boss. She was a sincere, warm-hearted, pretty girl who was genuinely in love with Matt. To the day of her death she had been a gentle, unaggressive person with an appreciation of the best in literature and music. The marriage served a purpose as far as Matt was concerned. His father-in-law had taken him under his wing and before long Matt was maneuvering for himself. The wide range of politics fascinated him; the real power was in running the machine. You could buy and sell influence, protection. You could wink at legal statutes; you could be a "lawyer" without practicing law; you could be a fixer without the public knowing about it.

Now at forty, Matthew Trevins had become a political figure behind the scenes. He had money. He had power.

That he had been miraculously saved from death, Matt had already acknowledged, but now a pattern of haunting unreality was developing that he could not understand. Thoughts, particularly questions, were forming in his mind that he had never before experienced. Were he on land he would know how to cope with all this. But here, confined to an ancient freighter on the high seas, he felt perplexed, bewildered.

Nothing in Matt's background had prepared him for the simplicity of a man like Riis or Samuelson. Obviously Captain Riis was nobody's fool, a man who was both mariner and surgeon.

Matt came to a single and firm determination: he would, as soon as possible, put to a test this matter of reality.

Matt took his meals alone, rested, and became gradually attuned to the full movement of the ship. Days went by. The weather had turned sultry and sometimes the odors of paint and oil, the smell of the cooking in the galley almost sickened him. But there were periods in the late evening when Matt enjoyed the luxury of lying in his bunk and listening to the conversation of sailors outside his door. He liked to stand at the porthole and look at the wide empty sea; or follow the churning water in the wake of the ship; or watch the green-blue smoothness of the waves.

The Mount Horeb was a vessel of about four thousand tons. She was painted a chocolate gray. He knew that she was an old ship, undoubtedly had been battered by storms and blistered by fierce suns. He could not help speculating on her history: where she had been built, and by whom.

Matt was pleased when Samuelson brought in word that Riis wanted him to sit at his table.

The captain's table was occupied by the ship's officers and various members of the crew. Besides Samuelson, there were Dijinsky, a Russian; a Frenchman named Roc, chief engineer; a down-East Yankee, Ed Billings. They talked with an easy familiarity about the voyages, the years they had spent on the seven seas; they talked of the ports which for some of them held attractive memories: Capetown, Sydney, Port Said, Singapore, San Francisco, New York . . .

Matt had a feeling these were kindly men: honest, without guile; strong men—in body and in mind.

Before the beginning of each meal, it was the custom of the men to bow their heads while Captain Riis said a prayer.

The words were strange to Matt. He was told that the prophet, Elijah, to escape his enemies had fled to Mount Horeb—the birthplace of The Ten Commandments. In the solitude of that refuge he had more fervently than ever before turned to God in prayer. *"Behold, the Lord passed by, and a great and strong wind rent the mountains, and brake in pieces the rocks before the Lord; but the Lord was not in the wind: and after the wind an earthquake; but the Lord was not in the earthquake: and after the earthquake a fire; but the Lord was not in the fire: and after the fire a still small voice."*

Watching their faces Matt sensed intuitively the religious quality that these men possessed in their hearts. They knew something he did not know. It occurred to him that perhaps they had not always been of the sea; perhaps they had come across vast distances, each man separately, to this ship.

Early one evening Matt took a walk on deck. It was a warm night and the wide luminous sky was powdered with stars. He saw that the door of the radio shack stood open. He walked in.

"Hello there, Mister Trevins," the operator greeted him in a genial voice. "I've been hoping you'd drop in." He was a young man of about twenty-five, lean and tall. He wore dungarees, a faded sweater, and his face wrinkled in an agreeable smile.

"Thanks," Matt said. "I haven't seen you before."

"My name is Luke Allis."

"Do you mind if I ask you a question? Do you get many messages in here?"

"Yes we do."

"By the way, what's the name of this line?"

"The Lela Mitcham Export Line—out of Boston. It's not a big line."

"How long have you been with them?"

"A year."

"How about the others?"

"I don't know, Sir. I've never asked."

"I'd like to send a radiogram," Matt said suddenly.

"Yes, Sir."

"To New York."

Luke Allis produced a form. Matt saw that it was a regulation blank. He composed the words carefully in his mind before he put them down on paper. The message was to Rose Henry, addressed to his office at Madison and Fifty-sixth; and he said he was taking a trip; that he would be in Panama City shortly, and he asked that she cable him at once, care of the telegraph office there. He signed the message "Tom Craig," a name Rose would understand.

"You'll send this right away?"

"Yessir."

Matt put down a ten dollar bill.

"There is no charge, Sir."

Samuelson did not come to the cabin until late that night. Matt heard him but did not speak. He watched Samuelson standing before the candle, his head bowed.

Matt strained his ears but he could hear no words.

When Samuelson stepped away from the candle, sat down on the bunk and began to pull off his boots, Matt asked: "Samuelson, what does that flame mean, burning like that, day and night?"

"The light of the candle is pure; it eliminates darkness. It is, as St. John said, an enlightenment for those who sit in the darkness and in the shadow of death. Men have different ways of talking to God. By prayer, by meditation." When Samuelson finished speaking, he stretched out on the bunk.

Matt was touched by Samuelson's sincerity and the beauty of his words.

The Mount Horeb sailed past Colon, went through the Panama Canal and docked at Balboa. Matt looked across at the other docks to either side of the pier where the freighter was moored; there were some big vessels of American and British registry alongside the cement piers; from that direction came the loud, unceasing sound of winches, the cries of native dockmen, and the clattering noise of trucks and motor tugs running in and out of the warehouses between the piers.

Across the road from the Mount Horeb's dock there were a series of hills where quarries were in operation. The hills were rocky, bare, dust-brown; but at the summit they were green with the mango tree. As Matt stood at the deck railing, Samuelson joined him.

"How about going ashore with me?" Matt asked.

Samuelson smiled and shook his head. He was sorry, but the captain and he had some business to attend to; they were waiting for orders. "Why don't you go yourself—I think you'll like Panama. It's a beautiful city and if you have never been there . . ."

"I think I will," Matt said. "It'll be good to stretch my legs on land."

He was wearing dungarees and a blue shirt. He went down to his cabin to put on the clothes he had been wearing when he was taken aboard the freighter. Though it was still early the sun was beating down with a blazing intensity, and he knew that his flannel suit would be most uncomfortable.

Back on deck, he saw Riis. The captain nodded. Matt walked up to him: "I'm going ashore—it'll be good to stretch my legs," conscious that he was repeating the same words he had used on Samuelson.

"We sail at six o'clock," Riis said. "Try to get back in time."

"Thanks." For a flashing moment Matt had an impulse to shake Riis by the hand, to say good-by; to go back and say good-by to all of them. He gave Riis one more searching glance but noted nothing in the inscrutable face.

Matt left the ship. Up the road a little distance, by the big docks, three taxicabs were standing. The native driver of the first one saw him.

"Ride, Mister?" he asked in perfect English.

"Yes, sure, Panama City," Matt said. "How long does it take?"

"About fifteen minutes."

Matt got in. The taxicab headed east. He asked, "Do you know where the Western Union office is?"

"Sure. But we call it All American Cable."

"Whatever you call it," Matt said, good-naturedly, "that's where I want to go."

The taxicab sped down Roosevelt Avenue—wide, tree-flanked and beautiful. Hills of various heights, some of them very rocky, reached away from either side of the boulevard. The taxicab passed through Ancon, a small village, and continued toward Panama City.

As the city came into view, Matt recalled Riis' words: "We sail at six o'clock. Try to get back in time."

What did he mean? He had no intention of returning to the Mount Horeb. What he had gained from his life on it was good indeed, and he was grateful—to Riis, to Samuelson, to all of them—but now that he was well and strong again, it was odd that Riis should expect him to come back. Come back to what? To spend the rest of his life floating around on a freighter? To be caught up in a world foreign to everything he knew? There was nothing that could draw him back. He was no part of that strange company; he had nothing in common with them.

True, he had had a close brush with death. By a miraculous rescue . . . All right, by God's intervention. Good. He would pay tribute to God. He would donate a wing in a hospital, he would give money to the Church; he could and he would do a hundred different things to show that he was grateful. But go back to the freighter he would not.

He thought of the wire he had sent Rose Henry from the Mount Horeb. Well, he'd see if there was an answer. Surely, if the radiogram had been sent, Rose would have replied. Unless—Luke Allis had played a game with him. He'd soon find out.

The taxicab entered the city and made its way up Central Avenue to the telegraph office.

Without warning, a sudden tropic downpour slashed through the sunlight and Matt made a dash for the building. He got caught in the rain, but he laughed heartily at the physical reality that the rain had spelled out.

He went up to the counter. A young woman of Latin countenance got up from a typewriter and telegraph keyboard. Matt said pleasantly, "Will you please see if there is a cable for me from New York? It'll be in the name of Tom Craig."

"I'll see, Sir," the woman said. She thumbed through a stack of envelopes, stopped at one, drew it out and gave it to him. Matt took it with a glad heart and slightly trembling fingers.

He said, "Thank you," in such a surprised way that the young woman smiled at him and for a moment watched him as he withdrew to a writing desk and sat down. The envelope was not sealed and he pulled out the message eagerly. He read: ADVISED ALL PARTIES THAT DOCTORS ORDERED COMPLETE CHANGE AND YOU ARE ON HUNTING TRIP IN COLORADO. NO WORRIES HERE.

Good old Rose, Matt thought. He could always count on her to handle things. For still another reason the message was reassuring—his radiogram had gone out in an orderly way from the Mount Horeb. No hocus-pocus about that.

The rain stopped as suddenly as it had begun; when he walked into the street again the sunshine flared bright and the humidity was dense, enervating. Matt felt the uncomfortable pressure of the clothes he wore; but with the telegram in one pocket and money in another, he felt immensely wealthy.

He felt unusually light-footed and free, too, even though the humidity grew heavier, stickier. All along Central Avenue, the city's principal business street, there was much to attract the eye. Cabarets were not too far separated from smart department stores, whose windows were designed to attract the attention of the wealthier American trade, resident and tourist. The vehicular traffic was like a steady stream, the passenger cars chiefly of British and American make; and as he continued on his walk, noting the names of American business firms that maintained branch offices here, he began to spot his countrymen. At this hour of the day, approaching noon, they seemed numerous; for the most part they wore white suits of linen or seersucker. He saw some American women, too—they looked young, attractive, and they were also dressed in tropical white or light colors. It amused him to see portly, middle-aged ruddy-faced and seemingly cheerful Americans making for the bars like bees converging toward pots of honey. Matt imagined that the unceasing heat, the comparatively languorous way of life and the slackened business pace had toned down nature's otherwise aggressiveness.

Across the Cinco de Mayo Plaza he saw the International Hotel Bar and Restaurant. It had a look of newness about it, an-American-sort-of-look, and you had a feeling that it catered to the American resident in Panama and their native business associates and political friends. This impression was verified when Matt opened the door that led directly to the bar.

It was a long room, cast in a cool, soft shaded light, the humidity of the outside excluded, and made still cooler by a large electric fan placed high above a wide archway that separated bar from restaurant proper. About a dozen high stools with rich red leather seats ran the length of the bar; ranged about in an *L* shape on the opposite side were a number of dinning tables laid out in starched white cloth and gleaming silver. Each table had a vase of tall, exotic flowers.

Matt, after hesitating a moment, chose to sit at the bar. For a minute or so he tried to deceive himself that he was back at "21" in New York City. He had a feeling of well-being, and he took a keen pleasure in noting the faces of some of the men who sat on the high stools at either side of him. Americans, mostly: some with fat, reddish faces, and others tall and lean, who were laughing and joking in the way of men satisfied with their way of life and at peace with the world. There was something smug and carefree about all of them.

He was on his second highball, relishing the taste of the Scotch and debating whether he should order his lunch in the restaurant, when he saw that a group of three had sat down at one of the dining tables. One man was an American, the other a powerfully built Mexican in a suit of expensive tailored sharkskin cloth; and a strikingly lovely blonde woman.

Matt was surprised as he recognized Mario Gonzalez. For a moment, just to be doubly sure, he watched the Mexican as he spoke to the woman, his manner elegant and charming. Matt heard the sound of the woman's laughter, warm and throaty, and noted that she was indeed a beautiful woman. There was something about her that prompted him to think she might be foreign.

Just then the Mexican's eyes met Matt's. On the handsome and swarthy face there was first a startled, then an entranced expression. The next moment, oblivious to all other eyes and ears, Gonzalez' voice boomed across the intervening distance: "I cannot be wrong! It is impossible for me to be wrong! By all the tropic turtles, this is . . ."

Matt crossed to the Mexican. Gonzalez swept Matt into his arms, and while he held him with one hand he pounded him vigorously on the back with the other. Matt was a little embarrassed by this *abrazo,* but at the same time he was warmed by the lusty greeting and the glad, joyous feeling that he had found someone he knew, a kindred soul. For Mario Gonzalez was a promoter of a kind—always after a fast dollar.

"Matthew, baby, what are you doing in this place, Panama?"

Matt said, trying to back away from Gonzalez' embrace: "Vacationing."

"Vacationing! That's wonderful! What kind of vacation? How long? You are a man close to my heart. You are just the kind of a man I need, I been looking for. Oh, my baby, how good it is to see you." Gonzalez' words, filled with merriment, deviltry, cascaded from his Latin lips.

"Not so fast," Matt said. "I'm not shopping for a deal."

"How long did you say you are going to be in Panama?" Mario Gonzalez countered. "A week? Two weeks?"

"A few hours."

"Oh, no, you cannot do this to me!" the Mexican groaned. "And then what?"

"I sail."

"You sail where?"

Only a little while before Matt had sworn to himself that he would not return to the ship, but now he had just contradicted this resolve. However, he did not have time to puzzle over it at the moment. The Mexican's geniality overwhelmed him; at the same time he became conscious that the eyes of the woman at the table were full on him. He said, "Mario, I'm taking a sea trip—by easy stages."

"No fooling, baby! Pacific Coast?"

Matt nodded; he looked back to the woman.

Gonzalez was saying: "Come, meet my friends. Meet a beautiful woman. Most beautiful."

He led Matt directly to the table. The introductions came fast. The woman was foreign—Matt had guessed right. Elsa Foelger. An Austrian. From Vienna. The man was Tom Ryan, a resident of Panama and the head of an insurance company. He had a florid face, a balding head, sparkling brown eyes and a lazy smile. He was dressed in white linen.

Gonzalez said in his effulgent manner: "Matt's an old *amigo*. One hell of a nice *hombre*. Full of larceny, like me. Loves money like me. Beeg shot in New York."

Matt grinned. Mario's enthusiasm, although genuine, was

a little too exuberant. The Mexican pulled a chair from the table and motioned Matt into it. Matt sat down, facing the woman. He was conscious of her eyes—a deep blue, almost too soft and luminous. They studied him frankly, with no artfulness or embarrassment. Her hair was honey blonde. She wore a white sleeveless dress; it outlined delicately the supple rounded curves of her long slim body. Her lips were full. She spoke English slowly, fluently. Her voice had the tantalizing cadence belonging to the educated, sophisticated European.

"You are from New York. I envy you," she said.

"Is that so important?" Matt asked.

"Sure it is," Gonzalez interjected. "In a way, Matt, you are like all *gringos*. You take all the good things you have for granted. You have New York—it is nothing. Elsa would give her soul to have New York. She is *emigrante,* you understand? She cannot get into United States without proper passport or visa. Elsa, she is doomed."

Gonzalez hesitated. "Eh, Matt, you still got that beautiful girl in New York? That Senorita Morrison?"

"No."

"This is fine," Gonzalez said enthusiastically. "You marry Elsa and take her to your country. At one and same time she is both citizen and wife. Not bad, eh?"

Elsa Foelger seemed less embarrassed than Matt by Gonzalez's proposition. She showed no outward emotion.

"Elsa will make your life very exciting, very happy, very fine all around," Gonzalez continued.

Matt recovered and met the woman's gaze with a bantering smile. "I must admit that it's the best offer I've had today,"

Matt said. "What have you got to say to all this, Miss Foelger?"

Elsa sipped her drink, put down the glass. "Mario is my good friend. In his way he is trying to help me. He speaks the truth."

Matt smiled. "You seem very anxious to get to New York."

"Who wouldn't be?" Gonzalez shouted. "To be stuck here maybe for long time, maybe forever, maybe never to see America. Maybe someday you got nothing to do but go back where you came from—hell, Vienna, that's for beggars."

"Not you, Miss Foelger," Matt said. You'll never go back."

"You will help me?"

Matt stared at the woman.

"No," he said, "it isn't my kind of deal."

After a few seconds Elsa said, "You know . . . I like you. If you got to know me, I think you could like me, too."

So it was clear, Matt thought to himself, that she wasn't Ryan's girl. If she were Gonzalez' inamorata, the Mexican was obviously not jealous.

Gonzalez said, "I am here in Panama, waiting for a deal. While you think about the Elsa deal, I'll give you another. This one beeg money."

"How many deals are you working on?" Matt laughed.

Mario was always in some racket. A few years before Mario had brought a number of deals to Matt for his consideration. Matt had financed some of them. Two had paid off; the third was a loser. Gonzalez was a good businessman and tough in the clinches.

Now he had something "very special nice," he said. "I want you to listen good, *amigo,*" he added.

He linked an arm through Matt's and pulled him to a shadowy corner of the bar. He talked low-voiced, with persuasive phrases. The deal involved the purchase of four or five U.S. Government warships from mothball storage, their transference to the ownership-management of a Panamanian firm. Later, during an international crisis, there would be a "legitimate" sale back to the American Government. It was to be a "legal" outwitting (Gonzalez said it blandly, smiling all the time) of the U.S. Government in the matter of taxes. It would be a tricky and involved procedure. Gonzalez had lawyers ready to do the proper work for a piece of the deal. He needed a few hundred thousand dollars at once.

Matt's end of the deal, for whatever amount he put up, would bring him back many times the money invested. It was a proposition, Gonzalez said, he couldn't submit to many men; even those who had money to invest and whom he knew every bit as well as Matt. It had to be somebody with the right color of larceny in his heart. Somebody he could trust implicitly.

"I'll give you an answer in a couple of hours," Matt promised.

"Good," Gonzalez said brightly. "You stay here in Panama. I will show you how to have a hell of a good time. And money. . . . You like money, Matt. You always have."

A man approached them. He addressed Gonzalez with deference: "Sir, somebody is on the telephone for you."

Gonzalez left. Matt returned to the table. The Austrian woman studied him with quizzical eyes. Matt smiled and held a light for her cigarette.

"You are lonely—a lonely man," Elsa said after a brief silence. "I see it in your eyes, this sadness."

Matt looked at this attractive, foreign blonde warily. She had reached past his guard with feminine guile. "Why do you say that?" he asked.

She spoke frankly: "Because you do not look to me like a man who is on vacation. Much less a man enjoying himself."

"You may be right at that," he conceded.

She said: "I offer you something in return for something. I know we could be good friends. I could make up for some of the loneliness. You see, I have been lonely, too. And most of all I offer you sincerity."

"I believe you," Matt said.

"Thank you."

It was all so simple from Elsa's point of view, Matt thought. If only he had more time. . . . If only we had more time together.

"My ship leaves in a few hours," he said, finally.

Elsa leaned forward. "And you'll be on it?"

"I plan to."

"You are truthful but not very complimentary," she smiled.

Gonzalez returned to the table. He looked sharply at Elsa and then at Matt, as though from their respective faces he hoped to know their innermost thoughts.

Simulating tenderness, he said: "Matt, *amigo,* this woman I love very much, a deep and wonderful love; but because of you, the better *hombre,* I give her up."

Everyone laughed and Elsa said that Mario was the perfect friend. Tom Ryan, who spoke little, but whose expression toward the Austrian woman was one of adoration, said that since no one considered him as a rival for Elsa his masculine pride was sorely hurt.

Gonzalez and Matt apologized to him profusely. Elsa smiled and said that she was really attracted most of all to Ryan, but she had seriously weighed the fact that he was a married man. Whereupon the quiet and courtly Tom Ryan forgave her and said he would forever treasure the memory of her secret love for him.

After another round of drinks Gonzalez proposed lunch. Everyone agreed. A spirit of fun and banter swept over the foursome, and for the first time in weeks Matt laughed spontaneously. Gonzalez was a good raconteur and his hearty tales stirred Matt back into the stream of life that had been his in New York. Throughout all the talk he had a feeling that Elsa was appraising him, both as a man and as a potential protector.

Once, when he returned her study, she shook her head and whispered, "Don't think the worst of me, Matt. Incidentally, I think it is a beautiful name. . . . Matt. . . . Matthew. I say, do not think ill of me. My life has not been easy. I have seen much evil since I fled from Vienna, and I have kept away from evil as much as any woman can."

It was one o'clock when they finished their lunch, and Matt still had five hours before the Mount Horeb sailed. The thought of sailing receded as a definite prospect—Elsa Foelger intrigued him. There was about her a sense of mystery, a spirit of someone very fine, perhaps great.

Matt was delighted when Gonzalez suggested that they should all go up to his suite at the El Panama and continue their party. Matt said that he would take a room himself; he wanted to shower, change into fresh clothes. Since he had no other suit or linen beyond that which he was wearing, he wanted to make certain purchases. Mario wrote out the names of two or three stores.

Elsa said quietly, "Would you like me to go with you? I like to shop for men's things."

Matt asked, lightly, "Experienced?" and Elsa nodded.

Gonzalez said, "Matt, why is it you didn't come with baggage? I have an idea you took this trip in a beeg rush."

Matt laughed and said he left on the spur of the moment.

"I understand. Then Tom and I will be waiting for you at the El Panama. I shall get fine rooms for you. Okay?"

"Thanks very much."

Gonzalez made a telephone call and within minutes a chauffeur-driven limousine was outside the International Bar waiting for Matt and Elsa. Although the sun was high in the heavens the humidity had increased. A few minutes later they were in an air-conditioned haberdashery. Elsa helped Matt select two light suits, some shirts, underwear and other items.

Matt led Elsa to the perfume counter.

"It isn't necessary for you to buy me a gift," she said. "I enjoyed shopping with you."

"I want to buy you something," Matt insisted. "I mean that."

"When you buy me something, Matt," she spoke slowly, "it will be very important to me."

He looked at her a moment or two. "Just as you say." They walked out of the store and Matt helped her into the waiting automobile.

Elsa was also staying at the El Panama. At the desk, after Matt had been given the key to his suite, he found a message from Gonzalez: Matt would hear from him at three-thirty this afternoon.

He turned to Elsa. "I'll have a cocktail waiting for you in an hour."

Her reply was immediate, frank. "I'll be there."

The suite was "fine" as Gonzalez had promised; and Matt, standing for a minute or two on the large balcony with a view of the Pacific, felt a luxurious feeling of well-being. He took a leisurely shower, shaved, put on some shorts and stretched out on a sofa near the balcony.

The hotel management had obligingly provided an air mail edition of The New York Times and Matt, like a man who comes upon something precious that he had almost forgotten, picked it up eagerly. The look and size of the newspaper spelt in so many unaccountable ways everything he knew, had known— all the turbulence, the drama, the wealth, the poverty, the greatness, the cheapness, the glory that belong to one of the great cities of the world. A city he loved.

He would call Rose Henry; acquaint her with his plan to remain in Panama and outline for her the details of the Gonzalez deal. He'd tell her he planned to be away another month. At the very thought of this decision, Matt felt a grin spread over his face.

At the end of an hour he was dressed. He ordered a silver shaker of vermouth cassis. Ten minutes after its arrival there came a discreet knock at the door. Elsa Foelger came in. Matt's eyes grew wide with sheer fascination. She was wearing a dress of pale blue, full-skirted and slashed at the neck. She gave him her hand.

He said, "You are beautiful."

For a few seconds they stood silent, like two people who feel drawn toward one another and who hesitate to express the strange or trembling wonder of it all. She smiled and walked out on the balcony.

Matt poured two cocktails, followed her. She took one, thanked him in a voice so low he hardly heard her. Behind her the sea shone dazzlingly bright. The woman and the sea—everything else, for a moment, seemed extinguished.

Matt held his glass in a toast: "I wish you, now, always, great happiness."

Elsa lifted her glass. "Thank you, Matt." And then, "I don't suppose anyone knows the perfect definition of happiness—the most intriguing word in any language."

Elsa sat down in one of the chairs on the balcony.

"How long have you known Mario?" Matt asked.

"He is an old friend. What others say about him I do not care. I know that he befriended us, my husband and me, in Paris. He asked for nothing then—or since. He is gallant; I say of him what I heard him say once or twice about others whom he admired—*'un gran hombre!'* He is most kind to me, and there are—as you Americans say—no strings."

"I believe that of Mario."

"My husband—he too was *un gran hombre.*"

She looked toward the sea. "We had a wonderful life together—before the days of the occupation. . . .

"We had to flee our country. We went to Paris. We were very poor. We were angry, bitter, frightened, disillusioned. That was the time we met Mario. He liked us, and he helped us in ever so many magnificent ways. Then my husband died —and I was alone. I went to Argentina. Later I came here."

Into a few words she had telescoped the drama of her life, poignant for all its stark simplicity; but Matt now caught, as he had done once or twice while in the restaurant, that tense expression on the oval beauty of her face.

"May I ask you something?" Matt asked.

"Anything."

"You're very attractive; why haven't you found some guy —some man—preferably a rich one—and married him?"

Elsa laughed. "Do you know something? I've asked the question of myself not a dozen times, or two dozen times, but a thousand times at least. Why?"

Matt laughed, too. "That's what I asked: Why?"

"Only two or three men in the past years have asked me to marry them—once in Paris, again in Rio de Janeiro. Perhaps I should have married one of them. I didn't. I guess I didn't love either of them sufficiently."

"Does it have to be love?"

"Very much. I want to love very much the man I will give myself to, in marriage; I want also to have pride in him. That means a great deal. But you know what has been happening to me? Men talk of love without marriage. They want me for a day, a month, a year. They offer money—not their name."

"Men in America, in New York, are no different than they are anywhere else," Matt said.

"I don't want to go to America to be an adventuress."

"Why do you think I can get you into my country?"

"I think you can if you have the right kind of influence."

"I haven't," Matt said. "Maybe I could arrange to smuggle you in. But I wouldn't take that kind of a chance."

"There's one way—marriage," she said quietly.

Matt had a strange feeling of humbleness. For a moment he did not know what to say. Then he asked: "Why would you want to marry me?"

"Because I believe—I sincerely believe—I could learn to love you."

Matt was moved by her words and for the time being it did not matter if he believed in them entirely.

He lit a cigarette. "I've never had a woman talk to me like this. Always before I've done the selling."

"I'm not selling," Elsa leaned forward. "I'm begging. I could be for you mistress, wife, companion, without being called by any one of these names. I can see you want to believe me, only you are afraid. You have been betrayed. But who hasn't?"

Elsa rose from her chair. "I'm going now. Mario will be calling you."

"Let's see each other later," Matt said.

"I'll look forward to it."

"I'll call you." Matt crossed to the door with her.

The telephone rang stridently. Matt picked up the receiver. Gonzalez announced he was in his suite on the fourth floor and he wanted Matt to come up.

Gonzalez' suite was almost a duplicate of Matt's. It was Tom Ryan who opened the door. Gonzalez was on the telephone, his face beaming ecstatically; he threw a kiss to Matt with the fingers of his right hand, not for an instant halting his conversation which was in Spanish—a conversation punctuated with *Bueno! Excelente! Magnifico!* And finally, rising to crescendo, *"Pronto,* Alfredo, *Muchas gracias!"*

"He's talking to Alfredo Munoz, influential politico," Ryan explained to Matt. "Mario always works at the top."

With that evaluation Gonzalez agreed most heartily. His face was still beaming, his eyes were like twin sparkling coals of fire. He threw an arm about Matt's shoulder.

"My friend, my very good friend, Alfredo, has just arranged an appointment with Mister Beeg! Did you hear, Matt —the Number One! He wants to see me right now! Personally! And I am rushing to his residence. Alfredo will be in our company. He is pulling the wires to give us important name, backing, position with proper people in Washington—beeg business! Is that not good, *compañero?* Is that not *excelente?* We will now make much more than two millions! Forgive me for talking cheap before! Come on, Tom; come on, Matt! *Pronto!"*

"Come on where?" Matt asked, overwhelmed by Mario's excitement.

"I am going to meet Alfredo. Tom, you will give me a ride in your car. Matt, you come along for ride."

Matt offered a mild protestation but it had no staying power against Gonzalez' lusty insistence.

It took fifteen minutes by automobile from the hotel to the meeting place on Avenida Norte. Just as their car drew to a stop, another automobile came along, and from it emerged a short, bulky man with shoulders and head incongruously too massive for one his size. Gonzalez saw him, stopped. They shook hands and the two men hurried into the house.

Tom Ryan suggested that Matt ride with him to his insurance office, located in the heart of town. Matt said he would go as far as the office; then he wanted to stroll about the city. When they reached Central Avenue again, Matt got out.

He had not walked more than five minutes, becoming interested in the Latin markets, run-down for the most part, yet alive with native color, when he was caught in a new thunderstorm. Unmindful of the rain, rather enjoying it, he walked on a little farther, turning corners willy-nilly, and then the rain came down with added intensity. Bareheaded and soaked to his shoes, Matt stood in the plaza. The day had darkened suddenly.

Across the plaza stood the inviting portals of a vacant store. Nearby he saw a cross on the belfry of a small church. It began to thunder and then lightning bolted across the heavens. Matt decided to make a run for the store, when a voice, speaking English with a Spanish cast, sounded next to him: "I'm going to find shelter in that church. Why don't you join me?"

Turning, Matt saw a young priest—lean, tall, dark-featured.

"I'll take you up on that, Father," Matt said on impulse.
Matt and the young priest ran across the plaza toward the church. There were already about a dozen people huddled in the vestibule. When Matt shook the water clear from his hair and after he had wiped his face with a handkerchief, he looked around for the priest. He was gone.

The rain continued with unabated fury. Matt listened to the talk of the native people and with some interest glanced occasionally at their faces. He stepped inside the church and found himself looking toward the altar; about four or five worshipers were kneeling at the altar rail. To his right, along the wall and looking like so many large telephone booths, were a number of confessionals. In the air there was a heavy blending of incense and garlic and the odor of rain-soaked bodies.

He started to move back to the vestibule. Instead, he turned around as though for a final look at the altar. Last time he was in a church, he now recalled, was when he buried Ruth. Suddenly he was struck with a feeling of guilt greater than he had ever felt before. The Church, he remembered, called it Conscience. The silent intonation of the word seemed almost new, odd, to him—for it was a word he had seldom used. It was alive and turbulent inside him.

In a sweep of emotion, the past came back to him. Memory swerved him sharply, like the swift waters of a river rushing headlong to the sea, to the last few months of Ruth's life on earth; and he experienced an aching pain in his heart. Under the stress of this sudden emotion, he turned and walked out, swiftly, into the street.

The sun was shining gloriously. He started up the street, his pace quickening every second without his really being aware of it. Dilapidated buildings, stray gaunt-bellied dogs, a pedestrian or two, an empty horse-and-carriage, a roving taxicab—all these came within his ken, but he merely took note of them, vacantly, as if they belonged to another world.

Then another image, not new and not invited, came to his mind—the Mount Horeb. Captain Riis' words—"We sail at six o'clock. Try to get back in time"—came forcibly, insistently back to him. Even as he recalled them and tried to put them out of his mind, he remembered his vow that he would not return to the freighter, that when he had walked down the gangplank he had said a silent good-by to it forever.

Walking rapidly down a street, turning a corner of another, crossing a plaza or another intersection—without once noting the direction he was taking—Riis' words kept hammering away at him. There was no reason why he should continue with the voyage; and yet a possessive and compelling force cried to him that he should. Mario Gonzalez and Elsa Foelger symbolized temptation, alluring indeed, each appealing to a separate part of his character or nature.

He had to make a decision. Minute by minute a conviction grew upon him that if he allowed the ship to go without him his life would not be complete. Involved also was the matter of honor; a debt he owed the captain of the Mount Horeb.

All at once he realized that he was almost running. He looked at his watch. It was eight minutes to five o'clock. He realized he had very little time left to get back to the hotel and then to the ship. He did not know in what part of town he was. Everything looked strange and unfamiliar. Back streets. Small, open cafes where music sent young Panamanian kids dancing. There was no cab or carriage in sight.

Turning a corner which opened toward a main street, he saw a taxi parked beside a small building. The cabbie was asleep at the wheel. Matt had a difficult time rousing him. "Hotel—El Panama—hotel—you savvy? *Pronto!*" He waved a five dollar bill in the cabbie's face.

Mario Gonzalez said: "You know best, Matt. I do not understand and since you do not tell me, I will not ask. If you must sail, then I say you know what you are doing. Have no worry about Mario. I will look for new investors. It may take weeks but what is time? You know something, *amigo*—I love you—I will hear from you again."

Matt said, "Maybe, Mario, and I hope so," and shook hands with the gallant Mexican.

At the door Gonzalez stopped briefly. "I know too, *amigo,* that Elsa will be disappointed. Perhaps more than me. But . . . *quien sabe.*"

Elsa's eyes mirrored nothing. It was as though all the other experiences she had ever known inured her to disappointment of every kind.

Matt admired her more than ever.

"It must be a rare and wonderful journey," she said in her soft foreign voice, "that makes you leave us, like this, so suddenly."

For a few seconds Matt was filled with irresolution—the look and nearness of the woman, their mutual desire for one another, collided against the imagery involved in the words she herself had used.

She said, "Good fortune to you, Matt, whatever your mission."

"Good-by," he said. They did not move toward each other.

Matt turned. He opened the door and walked out.

"How was Panama?" Riis asked.

Matt, sitting opposite the captain in his cabin, smiled.

"First time I was ever there. I liked it—very much."

The captain said nothing.

"Would it have mattered if I hadn't come back to the ship?" Matt asked.

"Yes—it would have mattered."

Matt was calm; of free will he had returned. He looked at Riis. "What's our next stop, Captain?"

"Port City," Riis smiled.

Matt knew Port City was a shipping harbor on the Southern California coast, near Los Angeles.

Part Two

THE LIFTING OF A CURTAIN

The room was bitterly cold, even with the window closed. As he slowly stirred himself to wakefulness, he sensed that he was in strange surroundings; a cheap room, an old iron bedstead, a worn gray carpet, a chair—his suit draped carelessly over it. With a confused mind, Matt Trevins slowly realized that his emotion on finding himself here was identical with that which he had known when he awakened in a cabin on the Mount Horeb.

He pulled himself to a sitting position on the bed, reached for his trousers and dug a hand in one of the pockets. His money was still there. He stood up, crossed to the window and gazed out through the murky glass.

In the lifting daylight the street below was silent and empty. He pressed his forehead, thinking: Why am I here? How did I get here . . .?

45

He had no memory of the ship having docked. Between the time he had fallen off to sleep on the Mount Horeb and his awakening here in this room, he recalled nothing.

Matt washed his face, rubbing it vigorously. Then he dressed.

The key was still in the door of the room. Matt stepped out and locked the door after him. The hall was unlighted, but he could see a stairway to the left. He walked down two flights to the lobby: a dingy room with a few nondescript chairs and a threadbare carpet. The registration desk was at one side of the room and the only light was provided by a gooseneck lamp.

Matt rang the bell on the desk. There was no response so he rang the bell again. In a few moments a door opened slowly. A stout, middle-aged woman with a long face, sharp nose, hard eyes and gray hair combed stiffly back from her face, came toward him.

"Yes?" she said coldly, surveying Matt from head to foot.

Matt looked at the key in his hand. "Three hundred and eight—that's my room."

"What about it?" she said.

"Did I register here?"

"You sure did."

"I'd like to see the register," Matt said.

"Why?"

"I want to see it." Matt's tone was curt.

"All right," she said irascibly, "but tell me why."

"To satisfy my curiosity. Do you mind?"

"Even if you're a plain-clothes cop, there's nothing wrong with this hotel," she said firmly. "It's a respectable hotel."

She produced the register and ran her finger down to the bottom of the page. "Matt Trevins?" She glared up. "Ain't that you? That's what it says. Here, see for yourself."

There was no mistaking his handwriting. With amazement, Matt looked intently at the woman.

"What's the matter now?" she asked.

"When did I come in?"

"I don't know. It wasn't me who registered you. My husband did."

"Did I pay for the room?"

"You sure did. Say, what you drivin' at?"

"May I talk to your husband?" Matt asked.

"He's asleep."

"What time does he get up?"

"Say, what do you want to find out, anyway?" Her stern, hard face flushed with anger.

"I can't explain it to you," Matt said. "But, maybe, if I talked to your husband. . . ."

"Come back when he's up—about nine."

Matt walked out to the street. Even in the gray dawn the place had the drab look of the waterfront. The sea and the docks and the ships were not far away. But how did he get here? He had no recollection of climbing any stairs to a dingy room; no memory of the hotel manager before whom he had written his name.

Well, he said to himself as he walked through the early morning mists, I'm going to make sense out of this. I'll find the Mount Horeb and get down to cases with Riis and Samuelson. What had happened to him that he could not remember? Had he been in a state of amnesia? Now that he was on land again, was he supposed to forget the Mount Horeb? Was that it?

The lights of a restaurant blinking through the mist attracted his attention. When he came up to it, he saw that it was a short-order place. Its single window was so dense with steam, he couldn't look inside, but nevertheless he entered. The place was garish with light, filled with the odor of bacon sizzling in a large pan. About a dozen stools were occupied by men who obviously were dockhands.

Matt saw an empty stool at the end of the counter and sat down. The man next to him, dressed in Levis and leather jacket, said: "Chilly this mornin'."

"Sure is," Matt replied. He ordered coffee and doughnuts. "How do I get to the docks?"

"Walk a block, left; then turn west," the man said. "Seaman?"

"Yeah."

"What ship?"

"Freighter—Mount Horeb."

"Never heard of her."

"Docked late last night."

"Nope, never heard of her." The man gulped down the last of his coffee, put a coin on the counter and walked out.

Matt ordered a second cup of coffee. . . . As soon as he found the Mount Horeb, he'd get all the truth from Riis—and then nothing would ever induce him to continue the journey.

He wanted to get back to New York as quick as he could. Plane . . . train . . . It didn't matter! He finished his coffee, paid his bill and left.

It did not take long to reach the waterfront. The air was sharp and the mists were dissolving. Toward the east there was a bright glint in the sky that indicated sunny weather.

He swung along the pavement past a number of covered piers. There were ships at anchor but they were all larger in tonnage than the Mount Horeb. Above the entrances to the piers Matt read names both picturesque and familiar: Holland-America Line, Java Pacific, Matson Navigation Company, Standard Oil Company, American President Lines, General Steamship Corp. Ltd., Bakke Steamship Corp., Grace Lines.

Farther along he saw the outline of a vessel, shrouded in a kind of morning-gray, that seemed to resemble the Mount Horeb. When he came up to it he saw no one on deck. Above the pier the name of the company was printed in dark letters —Quaker Line.

Matt walked on. Once again he thought that he recognized the Mount Horeb in another freighter painted a chocolate gray, but it was called the Lombok and flew a Dutch flag.

A man walked toward him.

"I'm looking for a ship named the Mount Horeb," Matt said.

"Mount Horeb? Never heard of her."

"She's a freighter, out of Boston."

"What line?"

"The Lela Mitcham."

"Never heard of that, either."

"Do you know of any freighter that docked during the night?" Matt asked.

"I heard that a ship got in a few hours ago—Berth 228-E."

"Thank you."

Past pier after pier for a distance of about a mile Matt trudged. Finally he came to Pier 228-E. The ship anchored there was a freighter all right but it belonged to the Luckenbach Line.

Heavy-hearted, Matt was more determined than ever to locate the Mount Horeb. For the next hour he roamed the waterfront from one end to the other. At every pier he was given the same answer.

"Never heard of her," one and all told him.

Matt kept on. A few blocks later he saw a restaurant. The sea air and the long walk had given him an appetite and he decided on a hearty breakfast. It was a warm and bright interior, very clean and orderly. He chose a small table by a window and ordered a full breakfast with ham and eggs and toast and coffee.

The waitress put a copy of the Los Angeles Times before him. Matt thumbed quickly through its pages and found the column devoted to "Ship Arrivals and Departures." He read the names of the vessels—arrived, due to arrive, due to sail, and those that were inactive in port.

By the time he reached the bottom of the long list there was a sinking feeling in his heart of disappointment, of frustration, of bewilderment. He left his food scarcely touched, swallowed the black coffee, paid his bill and walked out into the street again.

The small lobby of the Port Hotel was still empty when

Matt got back. He rang the desk-bell and the woman to whom he had talked earlier came out and looked at him steadily.

Matt said: "May I see your husband now?"

"He ain't here," she said, "but he told me about checkin' you in."

"What did he say?"

"There was another man with you. You was both sober, my husband says."

"This man who came with me last night—did your husband tell you what he looked like?"

"Yeah," the woman said. "He was a tall feller, taller'n you I reckon—sailor-feller. Kinda dark face, dark hair, maybe foreign, but didn't talk like one." She regarded Matt fixedly. "Don't tell me you don't know who he is?"

"Perhaps I do," Matt said slowly. He was thinking of Samuelson. "Thanks."

The woman gave Matt the key to his room. He was half-way up the stairs when she called to him.

"By the way, there was a man here lookin' for ya, askin' for ya."

Matt turned to look at her. "Was it the same man who came to the hotel with me?"

"I don't know."

"Did he give you his name?"

"No." She hesitated, then went on: "He knew your name. He was comin' down the stairs an' I happen to be standin' here. I never seen him before an' I ast him what he was doin' here. He said he had been up to your room but you wasn't in."

"And he didn't leave his name?"

"I told you already he di'n't."

"What did he look like?"

"He was kinda blond," the woman said. "An' not too tall. Not fat, no you wouldn't say he was fat, but kinda big shoulders—sorta well dressed."

"Did he say he was coming back?"

"No."

Matt walked up the stairs and entered his room. He glanced around as though he expected to see a sign, a piece of evidence that would identify the visitor. He saw nothing. Who was this man—what did he want? No one knew he was in Port City other than the men on the Mount Horeb.

There was no doubt in Matt's mind that Samuelson had brought him here. The startling, the incredible, the hard-to-believe thing was that he had no memory of it; and the fact that no one knew of the existence of a ship named the Mount Horeb. Yet he was on land, very much alive!

Where was all this leading? Matt felt a momentary chill. He lit a cigarette. Fear—a sudden panic—seized him.

An hour later he was still in his room, pacing the narrow quarters. He decided to gamble another day before turning tail.

He went out on the main street again, had a drink at a bar, bought a package of cigarettes and two newspapers: the Los Angeles Times and the Port City Herald. With this reading matter he could wait, hoping the stranger would return.

During the brief time Matt had been gone from the hotel room, his bed had been made up. The sun was pouring in through the open window. He sat down on the bed and spread out the Los Angeles paper.

As Matt read through its many pages, he got a vivid impression of the colorful California metropolis: its social whirl, its movie studios, its political whirligigs. Los Angeles was no different from New York, Chicago, Kansas City, St. Louis, Cleveland. The familiar political charges of graft and corruption, vehement denials, affirmations of civic pride, fervent declarations on editorial pages that there was nothing wrong with the American way of life that couldn't be cured.

He read a Victor Riesel column attacking a labor racketeer, and a scholarly piece dealing with foreign affairs by Walter Lippmann. Matt couldn't help smiling cynically. Riesel's fervent rage and Lippmann's academic analysis of a question of statesmanship somehow failed to change or alter anything or anybody. Life went along as before; there had been Riesels and Lippmanns in equal division since man put pen to paper.

Matt thought to himself: Why isn't the world better? Millions of men had figured in two world wars and several international "police actions"; and a lot of them had died and a lot of them had come back resolved to make a brave new world. Who stopped them? What stopped them? Why did men war against themselves, against each other, both at home and abroad?

How had Hate become Global Enemy Number One? Why were men rushing the day of a nuclear ash heap? When and how would it all end?

Lindbergh, Matt thought, had said it best of all: "We have passed from the Indian massacre to the atomic annihilation."

Matt, wondering at the turn of his thoughts, put aside the metropolitan paper and picked up the Port City Herald. His attention was drawn to a two-column boxed editorial carrying the headline: LET US STOP EVIL IN PORT CITY!

Written in fierce, righteous anger, it was a blistering indictment of a character named Lemuel "Ducks" Moran, underworld kingpin in Port City. According to the editorial —signed by the Herald's editor-publisher, Clifford Jones— Moran's money had subsidized and corrupted politicians, businessmen, city officials. The editor-publisher charged that Moran ran a string of gambling places, had an interest in "protected" prostitution, and took a cut of every bookie joint in the seaport town.

So it was here, too, Matt thought, even in this little seaport town—as it was in a hundred other cities. Graft. Corruption. Crooked money.

He looked at his watch. Twelve o'clock. He felt hungry. He walked out of the room, locked the door, went down to the street, hailed a roving taxicab. "What's the best hotel in town?"

"The Hamilton," the driver said. "Pretty good for a town like this. Classy lobby, fine restaurant."

"Okay. Take me there."

The taxicab pulled up to the Hamilton Hotel. Matt paid the driver, added a tip, and went inside. Compared to the place he had just left, the Hamilton seemed indeed a palace. He asked for a room that faced the ocean.

Since he had come without luggage, he gave the desk clerk two hundred dollars in advance. And, most important of all, Matt asked the clerk to book him on a one-way, first-class flight to New York tomorrow night. He registered, took his key and went into the dining room.

The restaurant was pleasant, the service efficient, the food good. Matt felt somewhat released from the tension under which he had been living.

He went to his room and placed a telephone call to Rose Henry in New York City. A few minutes later the operator reported that she was unable to contact his party. Matt gave instructions to keep on trying. Then he placed a call to Mario Gonzalez in Panama City.

Gonzalez' voice came on the line booming enthusiastically. Amenities over, Matt said: "Mario, unless you hear from me to the contrary, I'll see you in about eight days."

"I don't believe it, *amigo*."

"I'm on the level, Mario."

"Are you coming in on my deal?"

"Is it still open?"

"Part open."

"How much do you need?"

"Sixty thousand."

"You can count me in."

"I need the money not later than a week," Gonzalez declared.

"You'll have it in less than a week. I'm waiting to talk to New York now and I'll give the instructions. How is Elsa?"

Gonzalez, for a change, spoke softly. "You have broken her heart, Matt. I think it is real—she is very wonderful woman. You are a fool not to appreciate it. Do you appreciate it?"

"Yes," Matt said. "Is she at the hotel now?"

"I do not know. You can try."

"Switch me back to the desk, Mario."

Elsa Foelger was in her room. Though she seemed thrilled to hear from him, he had a feeling that his call was not entirely a surprise. After her first exclamation, she spoke in that slow way she had—reserved, yet touched with an intangible and haunting sincerity.

"Matt, hear a confession. I prayed that you would be talking to me like this. I am not ashamed to tell you. I am not trying to be subtle."

"I'll be in Panama in a week," Matt said.

"This, too, I prayed for."

"I'm in Port City now. From here I go to New York. I'll be there a couple of days and then fly to Panama."

"When do you leave for New York?"

"Tomorrow night."

"Matt, listen to me. I will love you my whole life."

For a long time after he put down the telephone, his thoughts were only of Elsa Foelger—who was waiting for him. She meant something to him, something very real and warm. There was a quality about her that was wholesome, for all the sadness she had known; the cruelties she must have seen. . . .

The telephone rang. The operator told him New York was on the line.

Rose Henry was delighted to hear from him. Matt told her he would be leaving Los Angeles tomorrow night. He asked her to be at his apartment around nine the following morning. She should bring him up to date on all matters requiring his personal attention; have the papers that needed his signature; and, above all, he wanted her to have a hundred thousand dollars with her.

"I sure will be glad to see you," Rose said.

"Same here. How would you like a trip to Panama City? You can take your husband. . . ."

"I'll buy that," Rose said brightly. "Thanks."

So far so good, Matt thought. He stretched out on the bed and fell asleep.

Twilight had fallen when he awakened. Instantly every sensitivity in him became alive with the compulsion that he should hurry to the Port Hotel. He rubbed the sleep from his eyes, put on his coat, and when he got down to the street he took a taxi. Five minutes later he was at the waterfront hotel.

Crossing the lobby, he was hailed by the manager's wife.

"That feller—he's waitin' for ya—in your room."

Matt walked up the stairs slowly, turned down the hall, hesitated before the door and then entered.

The stranger was sitting in a chair by the window. At the sound of the door opening, he rose and said, "Hello," extending his hand.

Matt said, "Hello," in turn and shook hands.

The man's round, fair-skinned face was wreathed in a cherubic smile. He was of little more than medium height. He wore a white shirt, tie, and a dark suit. His eyes were blue, set wide apart under a broad forehead. Matt judged him to be about fifty years of age. He looked like a small-town merchant, Matt thought, possibly of Scandinavian extraction— Swede or Dane.

"My name is Ericson, John Ericson."

"I'm Matt Trevins."

"Yes, I know."

"How do you know my name?"

"Because you came off the Mount Horeb."

Matt gave the man a sharp look. "Do you know Samuelson?"

"Yes."

"You saw him?" Matt pressed.

"Yes—after the ship docked early this morning."

"You *saw* the ship?" Matt's voice was demanding.

"Yes. I was at the dock to meet Captain Riis and Samuelson."

"Nobody else on the waterfront saw the ship," Matt said. "There is no record of a ship named the Mount Horeb."

Ericson smiled. "The proof is—you are here. Riis and Samuelson told me a good deal about you."

"Why?"

"They were following orders."

The pervasive intangibility in Ericson's words nettled Matt.

"What do you people want of me?" He spoke harshly, almost hating the other's cool demeanor.

"I would say—we have a job to do; a job that came into being from the moment you cried out for help, back in New York. Above everything else you asked for a second chance. You received a great gift—Life!"

Ericson's words stunned Matt into silence. Frantically, in his mind, he sought an anchorage, a spar to hold onto.

He reached out toward the gleaming lights of Panama City, Elsa Foelger, Gonzalez. He tried to imprison the sense of hard pavements, dusty back streets, blazing sun; the El Panama Hotel, the soul-and-body allurement of the Austrian woman, the exuberance of the Mexican promoter. He reminded himself that he had made plans to leave for New York tomorrow night—then Panama. It might even be healthier all around, he thought now, if he left tonight!

Matt picked up his luggage and turned to Ericson. "I've moved. I'm staying at the Hotel Hamilton."

Ericson fell into step beside Matt. "Will you have dinner with me tonight?"

"You're on," Matt said with a grin.

They had gone through most of their dinner, and only toward the end did Ericson talk about himself, his early background.

He had married when he was quite young and of this happy union there was born an only child, Paul, in whom Ericson invested his pride and faith.

He was a boy of singular character; his mind attuned to both the beauty and the love of the world he saw about him.

When Paul graduated from the University of Wisconsin, the big guns were roaring; a great dark covered stretches of the earth. The United States came into the war, and Paul enlisted in the U.S. Army. He served in the African campaign, fought on the beaches of Normandy.

On the day of Paul's twenty-fourth birthday, Ericson received word that his son had been killed by enemy fire.

From bitterness and disillusionment Ericson turned to prayer.

One night, like a great exaltation, he knew beyond doubt that Paul was a symbol in the infinite plan and that he could never be lost, never die.

The next morning, while taking a walk, he saw Paul—walking beside him. He heard Paul's voice: "I am with you now, Dad. I shall always be with you."

Ericson realized again that no man ever loses that which he loves. This is the miracle of life. This is continuity; immortality. Even in suffering and in misunderstanding, in sadness or in the pain of disillusionment, Man rises above himself, above the meanness of life—touches Godhead—gathers new strength and direction so that life has a new purpose.

"I wanted to bring this newly found knowledge and faith to those who, like myself, need help."

Ericson paused, then continued: "I felt I must give up everything I owned, and this I did—my business, real estate holdings, everything. I said good-by to every member of my family and all of my friends.

"I traveled the world in search of the Truth as Christ preached it in the Beatitudes—the most inspired words ever spoken. I have stood many times by the Horns of Hattin, the Twin Mounts near Galilee where Christ gave his sermons almost twenty centuries ago.

"I have learned that Man talks to God, but more important, God talks with Man. God keeps open house. He is always here for Man to accept as a gift. We are never alone and we need not be afraid."

Matt had listened quietly to Ericson's story but now, he thought, it was time to try to put the pieces together.

"You've had a different kind of life and a very interesting one," Matt said, "but how do I fit into all this? Is there any special reason why I should have ended up here in Port City?"

"Yes, there is a man here who needs help," Ericson began enthusiastically. "Even more, he needs your kind of advice and the hard, raw courage which you can give to him. It is my hope that you will meet with him."

"When?"

"As soon as possible."

"What's his name?" Matt asked.

"Clifford Jones. He is the publisher and editor of a newspaper here in Port City."

Matt rubbed his cheek and then the back of his neck with his left hand—an instinctive gesture when he felt something tensing up inside. The gesture occurred only when the image or incident that evoked it was very grave or startling. And always it was accompanied with a sort of fear that took cold possession of him. He had it now.

He became aware of the silence that had fallen over Ericson and himself.

"Do you know this man Jones?" Matt asked finally.

Ericson shook his head. "Not personally, no."

"But you know he is in some kind of trouble? Needs help? And *I* can help him?"

Ericson nodded.

"Suppose I decide not to see him—or try to help him?"

Ericson studied Matt for a moment. "That is entirely up to you," he said quietly.

Matt's initial resurgence at being led into a suitation not of his own choosing was stilled by Ericson's candid reply. He smiled despite himself. "In other words, it would be all right if I go through with my plan to leave for New York tomorrow night." It was a declaration, not a question.

"Yes. There is nothing and no one to stop you."

"This man, Clifford Jones—is he someone I should know?"

"You knew his father—Al Jones."

Matt was shaken. Ericson had torn aside the scar tissue from an old memory. "I did a great injustice to Al Jones." He paused for a moment and then asked, "Will you come and see Jones with me?"

"No," Ericson stood up and put out his hand. "I am going to say good-by to you now."

Matt rose and shook hands.

"God bless you," Ericson said. Then he turned and walked away.

Matt sat down again and watched him leave the restaurant. The lights in the room, the tables with their diners, the murmur of conversation, a sudden burst of laughter, came into his consciousness. Listening to Ericson, everything and everyone in the dining room had lost their reality.

Unease drove him to take a long walk about the busy streets. He returned to the Hamilton Hotel, bought an early edition of the Los Angeles Times, sat down in the lobby to read, gave it up finally and went upstairs to his room.

There is one thing I must do at once, and then perhaps I can make up my mind, Matt said to himself. I must see this Clifford Jones, talk with him.

He found the name of Clifford Jones in the telephone book, wrote down the address, went downstairs, hailed a taxicab and in less than ten minutes the cab was turning into a tree-shaded avenue lined with modest homes. The driver slowed down to catch a house number.

Ahead a little distance, Matt saw two men hurrying across the lawn of a house toward a waiting limousine. The two men got in and the car sped away. With surprise Matt realized his taxicab was stopping before the same house from which the two men had come. He paid the driver, looked up and down the empty, quiet street, and then walked up the steps slowly.

It was a two-story house of wood and stucco; a light shone in the front room. For a minute or two no one answered the bell, and just as Matt was about to press the button again the door opened, and a woman stood in the doorway.

She was about thirty, slim and of medium height, with sparkling brown eyes. She had an attractive round face and her hair was short, soft brown.

"Yes?" she said in a strained voice.

"I would like to see Mr. Clifford Jones."

There was a slight hesitation and then she said, "Will you please tell me what you want to see him about? I am Mrs. Jones."

Matt gave her his name, said he had never met her husband but that he had been advised by a "friend" to see him.

The woman studied him for a moment and then said quietly, "Will you come in, please." She stood aside, closed the door after Matt and led him into a brightly-lighted living room.

A man was standing there, waiting.

Matt introduced himself and extended his hand. Jones gave him a friendly shake. Matt took him to be on the older side of thirty. His eyes regarded Matt with a fixed, intently-questioning but not unfriendly appraisal. He was tall with broad shoulders and a thick shock of dark brown hair, carelessly combed. He looked to Matt like a hard working but affable editor.

"Trevins," Jones said. "My father knew a Matthew Trevins in New York. He . . ." Jones stopped suddenly. "Are you the Matt Trevins my father knew?"

"Yes."

"Please sit down," Jones said politely.

Matt glanced quickly around the room. All the furnishings were in simple good taste; the room possessing a neat, wholesome look.

Matt said, "I want you to know that I am here as a friend. For the time being, will you please put out of your mind any feeling of antagonism you may have toward me?"

"I assure you . . . I have none," Jones said.

The atmosphere thawed appreciably. Matt said: "I happened to see two men leaving here just as I arrived. I have a hunch one of them was Ducks Moran."

"Yes," Jones was surprised.

"I read your editorial and I just took a guess," Matt said. He saw an exchange of glances between Jones and his wife. Then he continued: "A friend of mine told me you are in serious trouble and that I could help."

"What kind of help—did he say?" Mrs. Jones asked.

"No, he wasn't specific." Matt looked at Jones. "Suppose you tell me."

Jones glanced at Matt. "Have you a good deal of money?"

"Enough."

"Money might help," Jones said.

Matt smiled. Already part of a prospective battle line was coming into focus. "Let me get something straight. This Moran—how powerful is he?" The clipped phrases came naturally to his lips; they stemmed out of habit.

"From the lowliest policeman to the biggest politicians."

"Has he threatened you?"

"He is going to shut down my paper. You can't fight an enemy if he holds all the cards and can make good his threats."

Mrs. Jones put a hand on her husband's arm, gently. She looked at Matt.

"I think my husband is a great man, a man who wants to be of service to the people in his community. To fight evil, however, I suppose you must have something more than . . . well, plain courage. Nights and days unending, I've been afraid. I confess it."

Jones was watching his wife with an expression of great anxiety. "They wouldn't dare to do anything to them," he said.

"How do you know?" The woman turned from her husband to Matt. "We have two children. We're afraid that something might happen to them. It's happened to children in other towns—whose parents have refused to buckle down to underworld demands. It happened not long ago to the children of a newspaper editor in Illinois. Perhaps you read about that case. No one can prove a thing. A child crossing the street—suddenly he is run down. A child riding a bicycle

—suddenly a car sideswipes him, races on—leaving an injured body. Nobody sees anything; nobody can prove anything."

For a minute no one spoke. The woman's words seemed to vibrate in the room.

Matt turned to Jones. "Has he done anything to you yet?"

"A couple of his men. One night they waylaid me. I was hospitalized a week. I couldn't identify anybody. The police made a few arrests. But it came to nothing."

"How much have you got on him?"

"Plenty. Everything substantiated, checked, double-checked. And he knows I'm about to publish it."

Matt was grim. "I know how a man like Moran thinks and how he operates. Maybe I *can* be of some help."

"Why would you want to get involved in this?" Jones asked.

The two men looked into each other's eyes, searchingly. Then Matt spoke: "Because once, a long time ago, I knew your father in New York. We had some business dealings; no need to go into details. Anyway, I got rough. You see, in my own way, I was as bad, as corrupt as Moran."

Matt was thoughtful for a moment, then he said, "Fill me in on the details of this Moran thing."

Over the past two years, since he had acquired the newspaper, Jones said he had borrowed heavily from a title and mortgage company. The paper had tough sledding but Jones' faith in it was steadfast. He moved it up from a semi-weekly to a daily.

During his investigation of graft and corruption he learned that one Lemuel "Ducks" Moran had manipulated not only the strings of the underworld in Port City, but that he had muscled into the legitimate business life of the community, including control of the title and mortgage firm to which Jones owed seventy thousand dollars.

This astounding revelation, backed by threats, had been made clear to him only an hour before—when Moran and an aide had visited the house. Moran's terms were simple: Jones was to stop his attack against Moran; destroy all evidence concerning city and county officials who permitted gambling houses, prostitution and other vices to flourish in the city and county. If Jones failed to comply immediately, Moran would take over the paper. And further, Moran would disclose facts concerning Alfred Jones, Cliff's father, who himself had been connected with the underworld.

Jones had been pacing the floor as he talked. He paused, looked at Matt: "You know, of course, that my father served a term in a state prison. . . ."

Matt cut him short. "He wasn't guilty. As I recall, he was a young C.P.A. After his parole he tried to live honestly. And he did, and he was all right—until he got mixed up with people like me."

Mrs. Jones sat by her husband's side. Jones was gazing straight ahead.

After a minute, Matt said: "This paper of yours. It means a great deal to you."

Jones nodded. "Not because I am ambitious to be recognized as a publisher or editor. But I've been through a war. There isn't a man who has come home from any war without a changed outlook on life—and death. I am no smarter than the next, but in my kind of job I have an obligation to the public. When men like Moran are dirtying up our decent way of life and getting away with it; when public officials wink at social and political cancers and connive to profit by them— you have to try to do something about it. That's why I don't want my paper to go under."

Cliff Jones got up, found a cigarette, lit it. He looked at Matt and his grin was almost boyish. Matt's heart went out to him.

"I don't mean to be carried away by my own eloquence," Jones said apologetically, "but I've tried to explain why a free press must remain free."

"You've done a good job," Matt said and rose to go. "I'll be in touch with you." He shook hands with Jones and his wife and left.

Matt got back to the hotel and went at once to his room. He turned on the light, then turned it off; pulled a chair to the window and sat down. The town spread out before him in a myriad array of lights.

Straight ahead he could see the ocean, could breathe the tang and cold and mystery of it. He saw the lights of three ships where two had been that day. There was a sense of the eerie about it all. He could not tell why. Two were obviously tankers—the third, very brightly lighted, had the silhouette of a freighter, but he could not be sure. Perhaps his mind, moving in strange channels, saw symbols in everything. . . .

Tomorrow night I'll be free from all this—on my way back to New York, Matt thought.

He would settle this Moran affair as quickly as possible. He wanted to help Jones, no matter what the cost. He looked at his watch. It was a few minutes past midnight. He put through a call to Clifford Jones. The latter did not seem surprised by the call.

Matt said, "I want you to take me to Moran."

"When?"

"Tonight."

There was a silence at the other end of the line. Then Jones' voice sounded distinctly: "I'll pick you up."

"Hotel Hamilton—I'll be waiting," Matt said. "Meanwhile, suppose you give our friend a call and tell him we're coming."

The Moran home was in a good residential section set off by a wide grass lawn. There were no lights burning when Matt Trevins and Cliff Jones rang the bell. An elderly woman opened the door and looked sharply at the two men. After Jones gave her their names, she informed them that "Mister Moran is waiting for you," in an undisturbed manner. She took the two men upstairs to a room at the end of a hall.

It was a long room, with a large window looking out into a patch of darkness. The room had wood paneling and a bright red carpet. On the walls were pictures of sailing ships, a Bellows etching, a painting of a New York street scene.

Matt took in every inch of the man who sat at a large desk in front of the window: a middle-sized man with a thick chest, wide smooth forehead and cold, yellowish eyes.

Moran gave Jones hardly a look of recognition and shifted his eyes to Matt.

Jones said in a steady voice, "Mr. Moran, this is a friend, Matt Trevins."

Tight-lipped, Moran motioned to two chairs. Matt and Jones sat down.

"You didn't tell me much on the phone, except you would bring a friend—Matthew Trevins," Moran addressed Jones in an emotionless voice. "I didn't recognize the name right away; but then I checked. . . ."

His eyes moved back to Matt. "What are you doing in Port City, Trevins? Big man like you, from New York?"

"It has nothing to do with you, Moran. That is, it didn't until tonight."

"And now it has?"

"Could be."

"You came here in Jones' behalf—right?" Moran queried.

"About the newspaper," Matt said. "Jones says there's seventy thousand against it."

"It's *my* paper now," Moran declared. "Jones can get it back if he pays me the seventy thousand, and if he takes orders from me."

"No dice," Matt said.

"Then we're all wastin' time," Moran said abruptly. "I'm waiting for a couple of phone calls, so I'm going to ask you both to blow."

Matt got to his feet. Jones stood up too.

Matt said, "We'll be here, day after tomorrow, twelve o'clock sharp, with seventy thousand dollars."

"No deal," Moran said.

In New York City, Rose Henry arranged for a transfer of one hundred thousand dollars to Matt's name in care of a Port City bank. Another hundred thousand dollars, following Matt's instructions, was deposited to the account of Elsa Foelger in a bank in Panama City, and sixty thousand to Mario Gonzalez.

When Matt had the cashier's check for seventy thousand dollars, payable to Lemuel Moran, he telephoned Cliff Jones to meet him at his hotel. They waited until ten minutes to twelve, then took a taxicab to the Moran home.

They were admitted by the same woman and once again ushered into Moran's upstairs office. This time Moran did not ask them to sit down. He was smoking a cigar. Its rich aroma hung heavily in the room.

Moran deposited the cigar in a king-size, spotless cut-glass ashtray. His eyes looked down at it a little while; then he began to speak:

"I'm seeing you this time because it's the last time. After this, I don't want to be bothered." Moran looked at Matt as one animal suddenly looks at another.

Matt said calmly, "We have the seventy thousand for you. You're going to let Clifford Jones alone; quit bothering him. You're going to sign a little piece of paper we brought along." Matt nodded to Jones.

Jones took from his pocket the cashier's check and a legal paper and put them on the desk in front of Moran.

"I'm not signing anything. Get out!"

Moran reached for his cigar in the ashtray, and in that second Matt had a gun leveled at the mobster's chest.

"Well?"

"I'll sign," Moran said.

Jones had a pen ready and Moran signed the paper which restored full ownership of the newspaper to Clifford Jones.

Jones picked up the paper and replaced it in the envelope, leaving the cashier's check on the desk.

Matt said: "You go, Cliff. I can see the cab from the window. I'll sit here until I see you get into it."

The taxicab, a bright orange in the clear sunlight, was waiting at the curb. Matt and Moran sat in silence.

Matt saw Cliff getting into the cab. He heard the sound of the motor, then the horn sounding twice, as though to tell him that everything was all right.

There was a flash of fire and smoke, and Matt felt a rip in his side; he had a startling feeling that the bullet hole was identical with the one he had suffered when Carlos had gunned him down in New York one night not long ago.

As Matt fell to the floor, he fired at Moran, who slumped across the desk.

Matt looked at the dead man and felt blessed that miraculously his life had not been ended by Moran's bullet.

He lay very still in the bed and watched the dawn through the window. A false dawn—an hour yet before daylight.

He thought that if he could get out of bed and outside the building and walk along the quiet, empty streets, no one would stop him and ask questions. It might all be a delusion and yet the feeling grew insistently upon him that it would be true: the Mount Horeb would be there in the bay.

He had rested well through the night, and when he sat up and shifted himself from the bed to a standing position, it was with a feeling that he was testing himself. His heart was beating slowly, but fairly evenly and without undue exertion. He listened to his breathing: it was slow and heavy, even a little short, a little painful; but that, he reasoned, was to be expected.

He dressed carefully in the cold gray dark, never worried that he might be interrupted. He went down the corridor quietly, glancing at the doors on either side. He walked out into the street.

Matt thought: I want to make one more port with the Mount Horeb; it will give me a chance to express my thanks, appreciation, for all that has happened—the answer to my prayer that night in New York; the friendships with Riis, Samuelson, and their men; the finding of Elsa; the reunion with Gonzalez; the meeting with Clifford Jones.

Toward the horizon the blossoming light of the new day was painting the sky with roseate colors. The wind whipped a sharp mist against his face, and for a minute or so, facing the sea, he drew into his lungs a deep breath of air.

I must find the Mount Horeb, he said to himself.

Matt saw the sun shining upon the clear blue water.

When he reached the dock, toward which his steps had led him unerringly, he saw that at the water's edge there was a small dinghy, and he saw the tall, straight figure of a man standing up in it.

Beyond him, farther out in the mist-shrouded sea, was the outline of the ship he had seen the other night alongside the two tankers.

He recognized it now—the Mount Horeb!

Matt stopped abruptly.

The man in the dinghy raised his hand in a friendly salutation.

Matt said quietly, "Hello, John."

"It's good to see you again, Matt," John Samuelson answered.

Matt offered his hand. Samuelson took it and helped Matt to step firmly and confidently into the dinghy. Then Samuelson sat down and lifted the oars. Matt saw that Samuelson was smiling at him.

"It's there now," Samuelson said. "Waiting. You can see it."

"Yes," Matt said.

He looked intently at the freighter, lying at anchor. He saw the men on the deck, and even at this distance he recognized their faces. Captain Riis, his hands on the rail, was looking toward the dinghy.

Matt raised a hand and his heart gladdened when he saw Riis' hand go up in acknowledgment. Then Matt's eyes went up to the sky. A gull was winging out to sea. Matt's eyes followed it. It grew smaller and then disappeared completely. Matt thought, I wish I could see where it is flying. . . .

The nurse walked quickly out of Matt's room in the hospital and summoned the doctor. They went back together and looked at the body under the covers and saw the rare, tiny smile that for a moment clung to the corners of the lips and then vanished.

The doctor pressed his stethoscope over Matt's heart, and after a long minute he looked up at the nurse, and said, "He is dead."

The nurse stood at the window. She looked out toward the open sea. For a little while she followed the dark outline of a freighter charting a course into the horizon.

THE END

*"I have set before thee
an open door, and no man
can shut it."*—Rev. 3:8